IMAGES
of America

BENICIA

The city of Benicia was named in honor of the wife of Gen. Mariano G. Vallejo. Her full name was Dona Francisca Benicia Maria Felipa Carrillo de Vallejo (1815–1891).

IMAGES
of *America*

BENICIA

Benicia Historical Museum

Julia Bussinger and Beverly Phelan

ARCADIA
PUBLISHING

Published by Arcadia Publishing
Charleston, South Carolina

Library of Congress Catalog Card Number: 2004110477

For all general information contact Arcadia Publishing at:
Telephone 843-853-2070
Fax 843-853-0044
E-mail sales@arcadiapublishing.com
For customer service and orders:
Toll-Free 1-888-313-2665

Visit us on the Internet at www.arcadiapublishing.com

CONTENTS

Acknowledgments   6

Introduction   7

1.   Benicia's Beginning   9

2.   Industry and Transport   31

3.   Prominent Benicians and Their Homes   57

4.   Community   71

5.   U.S. Benicia Barracks and Arsenal   93

ACKNOWLEDGMENTS

Beverly Phelan and Julia Bussinger worked on this book under the direction and recommendations of Harry Wassmann, museum curator and founder of the Benicia Historical Society and co-founder of the Benicia Historical Museum. The authors would also like to acknowledge Mr. Wassmann's advice and valuable contributions in making this book a reality. Our deep appreciation and sincere thanks to Harry Wassmann! The authors dedicate this book to the 20th anniversary of the Benicia Historical Museum, May 2005.

We would like to thank some organizations and individuals who have helped us in this remarkable endeavor—bringing Benicia's rich, historical heritage alive in these pictures. The museum was fortunate to have many supporters from the very beginning. Pioneers, families, friends, and organizations shared their photographs with the museum. We are very grateful to Diane and Harry Wassmann, Gladys Wold, Tom Hosley, Lenoir Miller, Steve DeBenedetti, Donald J. DeBenedetti, James Robertson, Olivia O'Grady, Richard Tipton, Norman Peltier, John Cody, Joseph Coney, Marjorie Stoner Elmore Collection, Thomas Benet, Fred Nickerson, Lowell Kunze, Kay Yokum, Frank Fiore, Alec Brown, Dave Stevens, Ruth Alexander, Peggy Martin, and U.S. Army photographs. Some of our friends are no longer with us, but our appreciation for their help will live forever.

Our special appreciation goes to the Benicia Public Library, the City of Benicia, the Benicia Historical Society, San Francisco Maritime National Park, Archives of the Department of Terrestrial Magnetism, Carnegie Institution of Washington D.C., and Rock Island Arsenal Museum. We would like to credit the U.S. Army and its former employees who donated many photographs to the museum collection and gave us permission to use some of them. Special recognition is due to Eve Iversen, Frank Webb, Fran Martinez-Coyne, Bob Kvasnicka, Shaun Hardy, Hugo M. Schauer, and Jerry Bowen.

The authors are grateful for the technical help (computer work, scanning, and CD burning) they received from Tania Borostyan. Thank you to Louise Martin for her valuable assistance in retrieving photos. We would like to recognize authors whose works were used as reference material for our book: Robert Bruegmann, Richard Dillon, Don McDowell, Jacqueline McCart Woodruff, Earl Bobitt, and Frank L. Keegan.

This is the first pictorial book published on Benicia's history. We have taken responsibility for today's generation and the generations to come. We would like to point out that some historic pictures in our collection did not have enough information about date, photographer/owner, event, person, etc. and we apologize if we did not credit the proper source. We also realize that there are more pictures on Benicia's history that could have contributed to this book. We greatly appreciate those individuals who have given us their treasures to let people know what a glorious town Benicia was and still is. Thank you to the board of directors of the Benicia Historical Museum for its support and encouragement. Sincere thanks to all of our friends who believed in and supported us during these challenging times.

INTRODUCTION

The town named for Dona Benicia, with its glorious past, has been rediscovered in these pages. One of California's best-kept secrets for over 157 years, the town is a hidden pearl lying on the sunny inland shores of the bay. In the 1850s, Benicia was one of the busiest seaports on the California coast, and it retains many of its historical buildings and sites, and notable historic architecture, as well as the leisurely pace and atmosphere of another century.

Benicia was founded in May 1847 by Robert Semple, Thomas O. Larkin, and General Mariano Guadaloupe Vallejo, and was named for the general's charming wife, Dona Francisca Benicia. In that year before the Gold Rush, the town already had 20 homes, and Semple maintained a ferry service across Carquinez Strait to what later became Contra Costa County. Captain E.H. Von Pfister built a general store on the waterfront, and it was here that news of the gold discovery at Sutter's Mill on the American River was first announced.

As immigrants poured into California, many stopped at Benicia and some stayed to found some of the earliest schools, churches, and industries in the state, including the famous Mathew Turner shipyards. In 1849, the U.S. Army also arrived, choosing that protected spot to establish the Benicia Barracks—the first on the Pacific Coast. Benicia and Monterey became the first incorporated cities in the new state of California in 1850, and Benicia served as its capital for 13 months from 1853 to 1854.

Already an established town while California was a sparsely populated frontier, Benicia had many firsts in the new state including:

the first auto ferry boat in the world, the *Charles Van Damme*, in 1916
the first American heavyweight boxing champion, John Heenan, "The Benicia Boy," in 1860
the first railroad ferry west of the Mississippi, in 1879
the first military hospital in the West, in 1856
the site of the first U.S. arsenal on the Pacific Coast, in 1851
the first steamboat built and run by Americans in California, in 1849
the first major industrial enterprise in California, the Pacific Mail & Steamship Company, in 1850
joining Monterey to become the first incorporated city in California, in 1850
the first town to learn of the discovery of gold on the American River, in 1848
the first public school in California, the Benicia Public School, established in 1849
the first school for girls in California, the Young Ladies Seminary, in 1854
the first Protestant (Presbyterian) church in California, in 1849
the first Episcopal cathedral in Northern California, in 1876
the first seminarians to be ordained as Dominican priests in California, in 1857
the first permanent foundation of the Dominican fathers in the West, in 1854
the first official Masonic hall in California, in 1850

the first law school in California, in 1855
the first bell cast in California, by the Pacific Mail & Steamship Company in 1850
the first public transport on San Francisco Bay, Semple's ferry in 1847
the first hotel in Solano County, the California House in 1847
the first recorded marriage in Solano County, in 1847
the first hospital in Solano County, Peabody Hospital, in 1849

Much of Benicia's history is illustrated by the photographs included in this book—much, but not all. The authors were limited by several factors, especially the fact that a number of people, events, buildings, and artifacts were never photographed. This is especially true of the first decade of the town's existence, when photography was rare. In some instances, photographs did exist, but were poorly preserved, or we could not obtain permission to publish them here. A specific instance of this were the U.S. Army photographs documenting the Benicia Arsenal, which were restricted for publication. We were also challenged by a lack of documentation and information on many photos.

Without the help of museum curator Harry Wassmann and some other witnesses of recent living history such as Frank Fiore, Frances Preissner, James Robertson, and Ron Rice, as well as dedicated volunteers Marjorie Williford (board member), Sandy Moriarty (board member), and Lorraine Patten, this book would have been difficult to complete.

We sincerely hope that, even with such constraints, we have documented much about Benicia's past here, and we wish you a pleasant journey through the unique history of this early California town.

One

BENICIA'S BEGINNINGS

This July 4, 1848 view of Benicia from the anchorage is probably the earliest drawing showing what Benicia looked like in its very early days.

This 1856 drawing of Benicia reveals the promise of a beautiful waterfront city on the Carquinez Strait. To the northwest are the hills of Contra Costa County and Mount Diablo while the capitol building is shown in the center. Benicia was the capital of the State of California from 1853 to 1854.

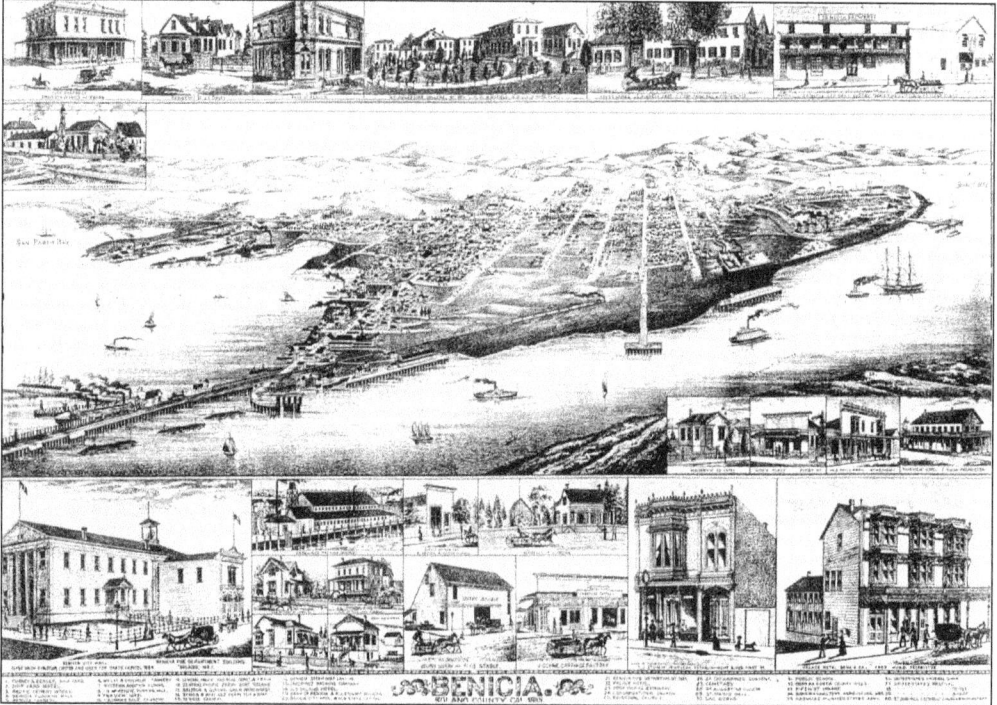

This bird's-eye view of Benicia in 1885 shows that the city was becoming an important manufacturing center. There were tanneries, canneries, creameries, equipment manufacturing, shipbuilding, and other businesses.

This view shows Benicia from the northeast in the late 19th century.

Business was going strong on the waterfront of Benicia by 1864, as shown in this view of G.W. Hume's Carquinez Packing Company.

This is a familiar scene on McKay's wharf where tanbark was delivered to McKay's tannery on the west side of town in the late 1860s. Tanbark in California came from the native tan oak tree, found in areas like Humboldt and Mendocino Counties. The bark was stripped off trees in four-foot lengths, left on the ground to dry, packed on mules or wagons, and eventually shipped to the tanneries. There the bark was ground up, put in large vats, and leached with water until all the tannin was extracted. The solution was boiled until it was the consistency of molasses and placed in 50-gallon barrels. The "liquor" was a concentrate to be used in vats or workers would use bits of bark with water to tan the hides. Tanneries in Benicia manufactured one-third of all the leather produced in California. Leather making was by far the largest industry in Benicia by the end of the 19th century and employed more workers than the Benicia Arsenal and Southern Pacific Railroad combined.

Mariano G. Vallejo, shown here in 1878, was born in 1808 during the Spanish colonization of California. A visionary who created an immigration policy that prompted Americans to enter Northern California, he was considered the most important Mexican official in California in the 1840s. Vallejo's military career began in 1824 as a cadet in the Monterey Company. In 1832 he married Francisca Benicia Carrillo and, after rising through the military ranks, became commandant general of California in 1838. In December 1846, he deeded to Robert Semple a tract of five square miles of his Soscol Rancho on the Strait of Carquinez to build a new town, named after his wife, Dona Francisca Benicia Carrillo. Vallejo was jailed for a few months at Sutter's Fort following the Bear Flag Revolt of 1846, and upon his release found most of his cattle and horses gone and personal property stolen from both his Petaluma and Sonoma homes. He died in 1890.

Dona Francisca Maria Felipa Benicia Carrillo de Vallejo was born in 1815 and died in 1891. A year after her marriage, a pregnant, 17-year-old Francisca journeyed approximately 800 miles from San Diego to San Francisco to meet her husband. At the time, she was the first non-native woman in Alta California. Vallejo originally wanted to name his new city "Francisca" for his wife, but as Yerba Buena was about to be rechristened San Francisco, the name Benicia was chosen to avoid confusion. Dona Benicia provided an exceptional home for her husband and 16 children and acted as a gracious host to visiting dignitaries.

13

Robert Baylor Semple was a talented man who practiced law and medicine, tried the printing trade, and even piloted a steamboat on the Mississippi. Born in Kentucky in 1806, he grew to be nearly seven feet tall, and friends described him as tall and straight with broad hands that clasped like a vise when shaking hands. He came to California from Missouri in 1845 with the Lansford Hastings party and was a lieutenant in the militia that arrested Adj. Gen. Mariano Vallejo in the Bear Flag Revolt of 1846. Semple later obtained 500 acres of the Suscol grant from Vallejo and with Thomas O. Larkin founded the city of Benicia. In 1849, Semple was president of the constitutional convention in Monterey, whose purpose was to draw up a constitution as the first step toward statehood for California. While in Monterey, Semple and William Colton established *The Californian*, the first newspaper in California. Semple would have been the first governor of the state, but was prevented from doing so by ill health. He lived out his years in Colusa and died in 1854.

Thomas O. Larkin was a successful merchant, land developer, financier, and the first and only U.S. Consul to Mexican California (1844–1848). He was born in Massachusetts in 1802 and arrived in California to join his half-brother, John Rogers Cooper, in 1832. Two years later he built the first two-story home in Monterey. In 1847, he became Robert Semple's financial partner in the new city of Benicia, but because his interest lay more in the cities of Monterey and San Francisco he dissolved his partnership with Semple in 1849. When he died in San Francisco in 1858 he was one of the richest and most respected men in California.

The first store in Solano County was an adobe built by Benjamin McDonald in 1847 and operated by E.H. Von Pfister. You could buy everything from brandy to hardware and fabric. It was a store by day and a bar and hotel at night. (The register from the store is at the Benicia Historical Museum.) In early 1848, Charles Bennett, an employee of John Sutter, and a companion were on their way to Monterey to ask Governor Mason to grant land, which included Sutter's Mill, to Sutter. John Sutter's orders were not to reveal the discovery of gold at Sutter's Mill in Coloma. Unfortunately when others at the store were talking about coal in the area, Bennett showed them his gold nuggets. The Gold Rush was on! Von Pfister left the store and went to merchandise in the gold fields. He returned to Benicia and operated the California House. His home is still at 280 East J Street in mint condition. The remains of the store are still at the end of First Street near Garske's Shipyard. Von Pfister died in 1886 and is buried in the city cemetery in Benicia.

The famous Washington House, located at the southwest corner of First and D Streets, was built in 1850 and is probably one of the oldest buildings in town. It was apparently built on East Fifth Street and then moved to First Street, where it housed a variety of businesses, including a hotel in the days when Benicia was the state capital, a speakeasy during Prohibition, and a Chinese lottery. Its reputation as a house of ill repute still lingers in the minds of Benicia's older population even though it was a restaurant for many years and still serves as one today.

The names Grant, Sherman, John A. Sutter, Col. Silas Casey, Judge Hastings of Hastings Law School, and many others appeared on the register of the Solano Hotel. The hotel was built in the 1850s at the corner of First and E Streets and was also the stop for the Pony Express before its riders caught the ferry to go to Oakland or San Francisco. The hotel was destroyed by fire in 1944. The site now houses the restored Jurgenson's Saloon, which was moved there from the end of First Street.

The spiritual side of Benicia's history began with the Rev. Sylvester Woodbridge in 1849. He organized a church of the Presbyterian faith in what is now the city park. Services were held in the first public school located on the site. It was the first Protestant church with an ordained resident pastor in California. Reverend Woodbridge taught school during the week and held a service on Sunday. A new church building was dedicated in 1851. It has been said that Reverend Woodbridge's Southern sentiments during the Civil War caused dissension among church members, which split the congregation and forced many to drift away until the church was abandoned in 1871. The building no longer exists.

16

Rev. Sylvester Woodbridge, pastor of the First Presbyterian Church, took an active part in the life of the town. He was a Mason and served the Benicia Lodge as chaplain, and he was a member of the board of trustees of the Young Ladies Seminary. Reverend Woodbridge was an eloquent speaker and was often called upon to officiate in churches other than his own. He moved to San Francisco in 1867.

In 1850, this Masonic hall was the first to be built by Masons in California. The lower floor served temporarily as the county courthouse until 1852. The Masons used the structure only until 1888, when they sold it and moved to a larger building next door.

The Union Hotel, located at 401 First Street, was built in the 1880s and is shown here in the early 1900s. Notice the corner entry. Originally in this location was the Solano House, which later became the Newport. It burned down sometime before the 1880s, and the Union replaced it in 1882.

The Union Hotel is shown here in the 1980s. The exterior and interior of the hotel underwent many changes in the 1970s. Additions included shutters on the windows, removal of the corner entry, and leaded glass windows. The most recent owners have reintroduced the corner entry and added an impressive sitting and dining area for their guests at this charming bed-and-breakfast inn.

Built in 1868, the "Alamo Rooms" has served as a private residence, a rooming house, an antique shop and a restaurant for railroad men. The establishment was also a brothel during the 1940s and early 1950s. An upstairs room was provided for clients with an invisible door for quick hiding. The building has housed several local businesses in recent years and is currently a restaurant.

The Benicia Firehouse, shown here c. 1911, was located beside the state capitol on First and G Streets. The bell for the firehouse was placed on the roof of the capitol building. In 1847, eight Benicia citizens formed the Benicia Bucket Brigade, which was the first organized volunteer firefighting organization in California. Today's firehouse is on the 100 block of Military West.

The Benicia Police Department took over the former Benicia firehouse on First Street.

Tales of Jack London come to mind when recalling the history of Jurgensen's Saloon, shown here c. 1900. In later years, the saloon was called the Lido, and a community effort to save the building was launched in the late 1980s. After 15 years it was moved to First and E Streets at the former Solano Hotel location. Currently, it has been restored and operates as a bookstore in the appropriately named John Barleycorn Building.

Writer Jack London is shown here on one of his sailing ships. This famous American writer made Benicia his headquarters in 1892 when he was only 16. Even then he had a weakness for alcohol and frequented the bars in Benicia, particularly Jurgensen's Saloon. He worked on the State of California Fish Patrol and possessed a machismo not common for boys his age. His adventures in the "Upper Bay" influenced his books *John Barleycorn* and *Tales of the Fish Patrol*. Benicia citizens at the time had no idea that he would immortalize their town in these two books. His last visit to Benicia was in 1914, only two years before he died at his ranch in the Valley of the Moon (Glen Ellen) in 1916.

The City Hotel is shown here in the 1980s. Originally constructed as one very long building at the lower end of First Street, it had to be cut in half in order for it to be moved down First Street between D and E Streets. It is now an antique shop.

The charming Fisher-Hanlon House was originally a Gold Rush hotel established in 1849–1850 and called the Ulalia House, located on lower First Street A fire damaged the hotel in 1856 and a Swiss-born Benicia merchant, Joseph Fischer, purchased the structure and moved it to its present site next to the Benicia State Capitol. The home was in the family until 1969 when, along with its contents, it was donated to the state by the Hanlons and is now a part of Benicia State Historical Park.

This view shows the interior of the front parlor in the Fisher-Hanlon House as it appears today.

Benicia Vedette

VOL. 1.   BENICIA, SATURDAY, DECEMBER 31, 1853.   NO.

This newspaper in 1853 was one of several that did not survive the passage of time. The *California Gazette* was published from 1851 to 1853, and the *Vedette* began in 1853, lasting only six months. These were followed by the *Solano County Herald, Benicia Tribune, Benicia Chronicle, Benicia New Era, Benicia Herald, Herald-New Era*, and finally the *Benicia Herald*, again.

23

After the turn of the century, parades played an important part in Benicia's social life. This Fourth of July parade at First and G Streets, c. 1911, brought out revelers to buy holiday fare and visit with their friends.

The California House was built around 1847 and may have been the largest of the 20 buildings located in town around that time. Maj. Stephen Cooper took over the adobe hotel in 1847, and in 1849 Edward Von Pfister returned from the gold fields and rented the building for $500 a month. It later became the Benicia Brewery belonging to John Rueger. After a fire destroyed the interior in 1945, large murals depicting Benicia's history were painted inside by a Vallejo artist. These murals decorated the walls of the bar and became a tourist attraction. The building has been closed for several years.

There's some mystery to the origins of this Salt Box house on West D Street. One story claims that it had been ferried to its present location from Port Costa. Today the house, which has undergone several additions and other changes, is privately owned.

In the early 1900s, the people of Benicia celebrated many occasions in the downtown area. This interesting side view of the Benicia State Capitol Building provided a perfect backdrop for them to gather and pose for a picture while waiting for a parade.

The Carr House, c. 1900, was one of the few brick houses in Benicia at the time. Originally lacking in ornament, with just the front block and rear wing, it was later enlarged and a porch and elaborate front door were added. It was torn down several years ago.

The founders of Benicia hoped it would become a Northern California metropolis due to its location on the Carquinez Strait, which connects San Pablo Bay, the northernmost extension of San Francisco Bay, with Suisun Bay. The land at the time was owned by Gen. Mariano G. Vallejo who was anxious to have it settled, and thus deeded a half-interest in a large tract to founder Robert Semple. So began Benicia's journey of growth and competition with San Francisco, San Jose, Vallejo, and Sacramento to become a major seat of power in early California. Even as the first legislature met in San Jose in 1849 and 1851, and in Vallejo and Sacramento in 1852, Benicia was hoping to become the state capital. A fine red brick building was completed in 1852 at the corner of First and G Streets for use as a city hall. When a flood in Sacramento made it necessary for the legislature to find an alternative location, Benicia was ready to lobby for the honor. It served as the state capital for 13 months, from 1853 to 1854. By 1950, the State Capitol Building was showing its age, and its Greek Revival elegance seemed to have lost its former splendor. A movement to convey the building to the state as an historical monument found favor with the California State Parks Commission and the California legislature in 1951.

After several years of research, the state began the repair, strengthening, and restoration of the Benicia State Capitol Building. The interior was restored and furnished in the style appropriate to its period of legislative use.

The restoration of the state capitol was completed by 1958. Returned to its former glory, the building is now part of the Benicia State Capitol Historic Park. Notice the sign for city historic designation on the left and state historic marker No. 153 on the right.

The interior of the Benicia State Capitol's first floor senate chamber has been reconstructed and restored with period furnishings and exhibits. Three of the desks displayed are originals from the days when Benicia served as the capital of California.

A period costume ball was held in the Benicia State Capitol Building to celebrate its restoration in 1958. Leading the dancers is Leo Carrillo, a descendent of Dona Benicia. Carrillo was also an actor in the 1950s television series *The Cisco Kid*.

Benicia mayor Ed Koenig addresses participants gathered on the steps of the Benicia State Capitol during the restoration celebration in 1958. The celebration lasted for three days and welcomed over 30,000 people from every part of the state. After the unfortunate loss of Benicia as California's capital and governmental center, a period of stagnation claimed the city. Fortunately, in the 1860s Benicia's growth resumed and the city began its climb toward becoming an important industrial center. With the arrival of the Pacific Mail Steamship Company and the establishment of tanneries, the city was well on its way to the economic successes of the1880s, when the waterfront included the Pacific Cement Works, Benicia Flour Mills, and the Matthew Turner Shipyard. With the coming of the transcontinental railroad in 1879, these industries flourished thanks to excellent transportation routes for their products.

Two

INDUSTRY
AND TRANSPORT

In 1850, the Pacific Mail Steamship Company chose Benicia over San Francisco to be its Pacific Coast depot and built the first large industry in California. In Benicia, the company made repairs to the great paddle wheelers of its line. Its workers helped build St. Paul's Episcopal Church with a ceiling that looked like an inverted ship's hull. Pacific Mail ships carried mail between the Isthmus of Panama and California. The company remained in Benicia until 1869 when it moved to San Francisco.

This image shows the bell cast in 1853 for the First Congregational Church by the Pacific Mail Steamship Company.

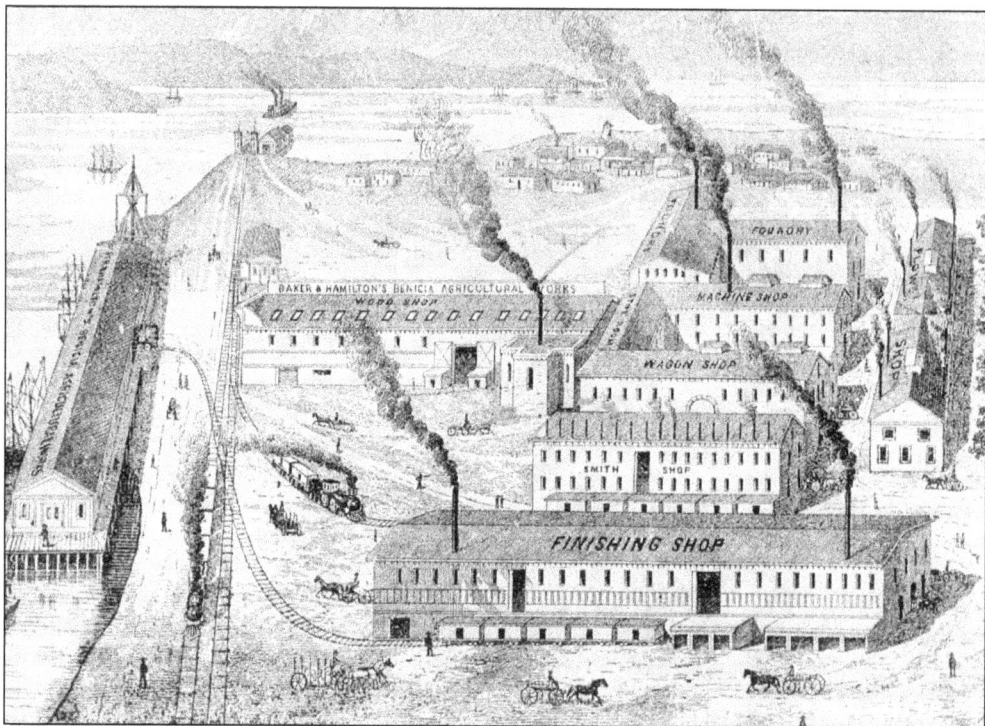

The Pacific Mail plant and docks were bought by the wholesale hardware company Baker and Hamilton in 1879, which changed its name to the Benicia Agricultural Works. The company's plows were famous as far away as Australia.

32

In 1914, Benicia Agricultural Works was sold to the Yuba Manufacturing Company, which built its own plows and tractors as well as Hicks marine engines. The company closed its Marysville plant and changed its focus to building dredges in 1929. During the 1930s, the company built 58 dredges, with the last dredge constructed in 1955. During World War II, the company made 155-mm howitzers. When the company met its production goal of 300 guns per month, it was awarded an "E" flag for production. In its last years, the company made diversified products such as dam gates, valves, water pumps, and girders for the San Rafael Bridge. Yuba Manufacturing closed for good in 1973.

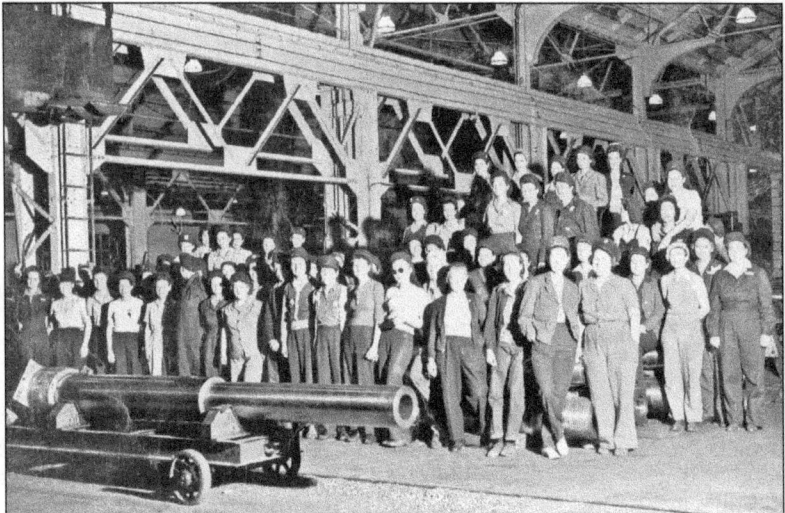

A group of workers is shown in one of the shops at Yuba Manufacturing Company during World War II. Note the 155-mm howitzer.

Pioneer Tannery, the first tannery established by J.R. Brown and Thomas McKay, became operational in 1864. Located on a site at West K and Sixth Streets, it was renamed the McKay

Benicia Tannery was built in the 1870s and was destroyed by fire around 1873. Soon afterward another Benicia Tannery was built by E. Danforth at the foot of First Street and was later sold to Kullman, Salz and Company in 1881. Operations were closed down in 1928.

34

and Chisholm Tannery in 1878.

Western Creamery was built on piles in the early 1900s at the end of First Street and was the maker of Isleton butter. The creamery closed before the Great Depression of 1929.

The G.W. Hume Carquinez Packing Company was the pioneer of salmon packers in 1864. The company also made fish fertilizer and packed fruit, operating well into the 1930s.

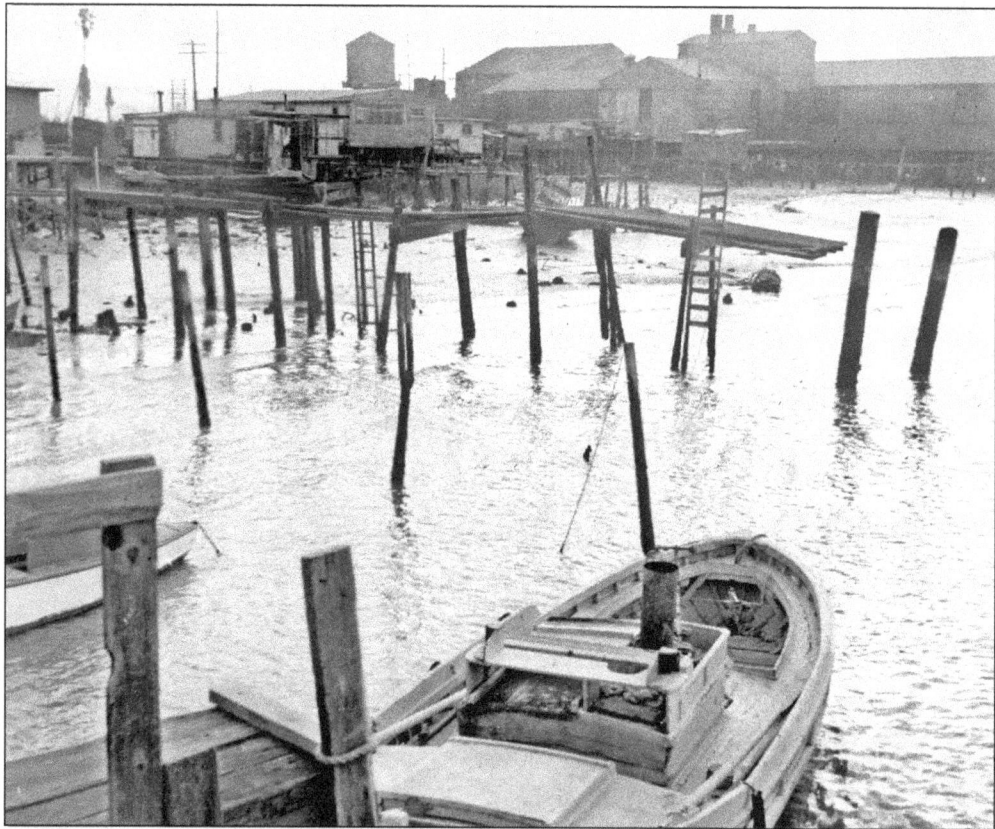

This scene near the Hume Packing Company plant shows the houseboats where the fishermen lived. Most of the early fishermen were of Sicilian ancestry, followed later by the Greeks. Commercial fishing for salmon and shad went on in the straits until 1955, when sports fishermen convinced the legislature to ban this type of fishing.

The *Scampo*, a 28- or 30-foot Monterey-type fishing boat with a Hicks engine, was built in 1905 and is typical of the commercial fishing craft that were prominent on the Benicia Carquinez Strait. The *Scampo* was donated to the Benicia Historical Museum by Capt. Joseph Garske Sr. In his letter to the Benicia Historical Museum entitled "Those Small Boats and The Men Who Fished Em," Jim Mortensen wrote,

As a young boy in Benicia during the 1940s and early 1950s I had an interest in the men and their boats that fished commercially in the Carquinez Strati . . . The boat had a very distinctive sound . . . and the men who operated this wonderful craft were very hardy individuals. They kept their boats tied in the tulles between First Street and East Fifth Street . . . [and] were mostly of Greek, Italian, or Portuguese extraction . . . Each year in the early spring most of them would load up their boats with food and clothing and head out on San Francisco Bay . . . through the Golden Gate and take a northerly heading for five weeks until they would eventually reach the fishing grounds in South East Alaska. Once there, they would fish for Salmon and Halibut for approximately six weeks or until the season ended. . . .

California's noted historian H.H. Bancroft called Matthew Turner the "greatest individual [American] shipbuilder of his time." Turner was certainly the most prolific shipbuilder in North America during the 19th century, having launched 159 vessels at his South San Francisco shipyard and 169 at his Benicia yard. A total of 228 ships were launched between 1868 and 1903. His ships, which were as fast as the steamers of their day, roamed the entire Pacific to Alaska, the Asian coast, Australia, and New Zealand, as well as to the South Pacific islands laden with all kinds of cargo, passengers, and mail. Turner was also a long-time member of the San Francisco Yacht Club and a charter member of the Vallejo Yachting and Rowing Club. Two yachts he built were considered masterpieces: *Chispa* and *Loriline*. During his life he was awarded medals by Queen Victoria of England and King Haakon VII of Norway for bravery in rescuing seamen during storms at great danger to himself and his ship.

Matthew Turner and his brother "uncle Horatio" are shown here at the Turner Shipyard in Benicia. These two men were considered the greatest mariners in California. A true humanitarian, Turner commissioned four new ships from his own retirement funds to help rebuild San Francisco after the 1906 earthquake and fire. His brother, Horatio "By Jinks" Turner, was a competent sailor himself, serving as master of the brigantine *Percy Edward* and other Spreckels Brothers ships. He left the sea to become superintendent of the Turner Shipyard in Benicia. (Courtesy of San Francisco Maritime National Park.)

The schooner *Solano* was built at the Matthew Turner Shipyard in 1901. The shipyard was located at the foot of West K Street between Ninth and Tenth Streets.

The barkentine *Benicia* was built at the Turner Shipyard in Benicia in 1899. At the turn of the century, with competition growing from steamships for the Tahitian trade, Turner began building big lumber ships to capitalize on the export lumber trade that was booming at the time due to the Klondike gold rush. Turner built for his own account the four-masted, 1,000-ton lumber carriers *Benicia, Amazon, Amaranth, Ariel,* and *M. Turner,* supervising their launching himself, as was his custom, and hopping about the yard with agility of a man half his age. In 1903, he retired from active participation and turned the management of his shipyard over to his son-in-law, A.E. Chapman.

The *Galilee*, shown here under sail during the last of three magnetic data-collecting survey cruises in 1907, was a brigantine built at the Matthew Turner Shipyard in Benicia in 1891. This "Pacific Queen," considered to be the most beautiful of all 228 Turner ships, was built for use on the packet line between San Francisco and Papeete, Tahiti. *Galilee* was very fast and set a record on her maiden voyage of 21 days sailing time from Tahiti to San Francisco. No other wooden-hull sailing vessel has broken her record to date. From 1905 to 1908, the *Galilee* served as the carrier for the Carnegie Oceanic Magnetic Survey party conducting research to correct the meager and inaccurate data of magnetic variations prior to 1905. The data collected during the 64,000 miles of her three voyages are still in use today. (Courtesy of Archives of the Department of Terrestrial Magnetism, Carnegie Institution of Washington, D.C.)

Matthew Turner is shown here aboard the *Galilee* in 1905. He was a pioneer of new principles and techniques in ship design. He reversed the old models and made ships long and sharp forward and lean and full on the water line aft. (Courtesy of Archives of the Department of Terrestrial Magnetism, Carnegie Institution of Washington, D.C.)

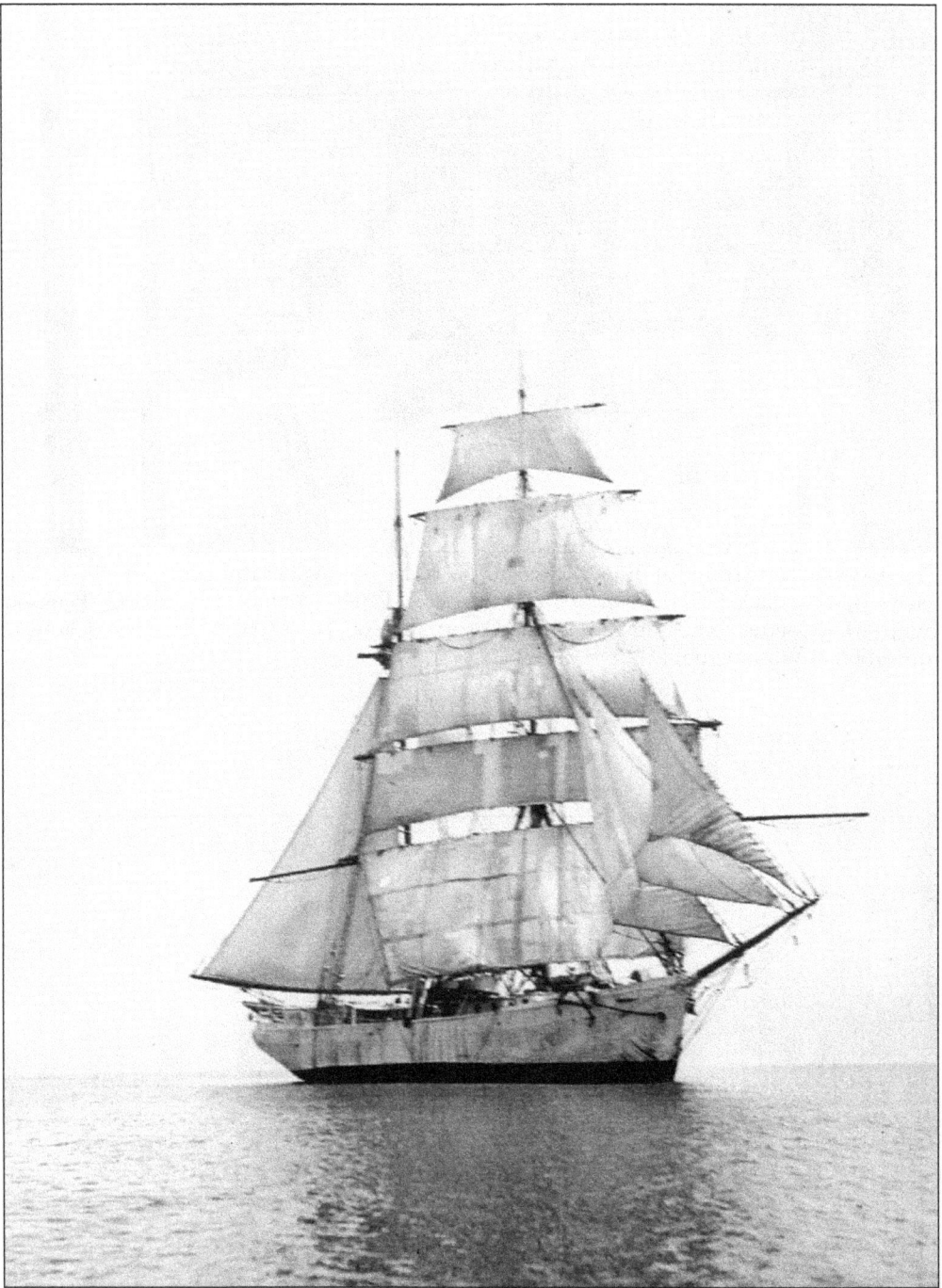

The *Galilee* sailed from San Diego during "Cruise III" on December 22, 1906, reaching the ports of Sitka (Alaska), Nukahiva (Marquesas Island), Tahiti, Apia (Samoan Islands), Yap Island, Shanghai, the mouth of the Yangtse River, Midway Island (no landing), Sitka, Honolulu, Jaluit (Marshal Islands), Port Lyttelton in New Zealand, Callao Bay (Peru), and finally San Francisco on May 21, 1908. (Courtesy of Archives of the Department of Terrestrial Magnetism, Carnegie Institution of Washington, D.C.)

The scientific party seated at dinner on board the *Galilee* during her third cruise in 1907, from left to right, included P.H. Dike, D.C. Sowers, W.J. Peters (commander), and G. Peterson (surgeon). (Courtesy of Archives of the Department of Terrestrial Magnetism, Carnegie Institution of Washington, D.C.)

The *Galilee*, shown here at San Diego, is dressed in honor of George Washington's birthday. (Courtesy of Archives of the Department of Terrestrial Magnetism, Carnegie Institution of Washington, D.C.)

Dr. L.A. Bauer, director of the Carnegie Institution's Department of Terrestrial Magnetism, makes magnetic observations on board the *Galilee* in 1905. (Courtesy of Archives of the Department of Terrestrial Magnetism, Carnegie Institution of Washington, D.C.)

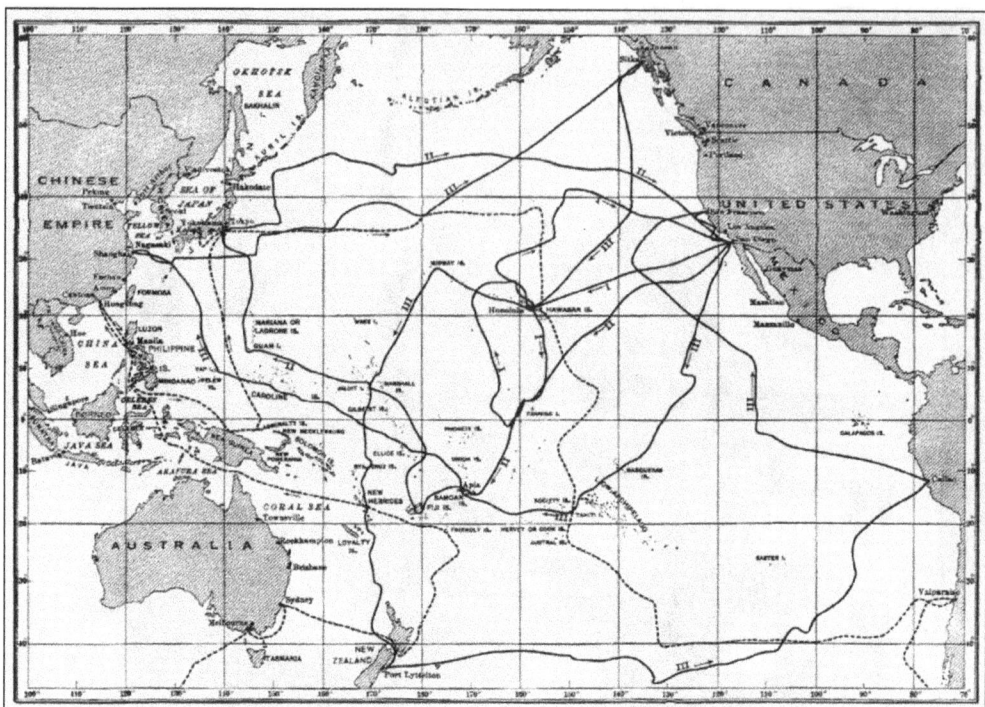

This map shows the three cruises of the *Galilee* from 1905 to 1908. Broken lines show the tracks of the *Challenger* expedition, 1872–1876. (Courtesy of Archives of the Department of Terrestrial Magnetism, Carnegie Institution of Washington, D.C.)

After the death of Matthew Turner in 1909, the *Galilee* was sold to the Union Fish Company, where she was converted to a three-masted schooner and received her first diesel engine. Until 1927, the *Galilee* was used in the codfish industry and two years later in the tuna fishing industry. She is shown here on May 16, 1931, two years before her sailing days ended when she was beached at the foot of Second Street in Sausalito, California. (Courtesy of San Francisco Maritime National Park.)

44

James Robertson expanded the Matthew Turner Shipyard and built a number of impressive vessels, including the auto ferry *Charles Van Damme* (below), stern-wheel ferry *Petaluma*, and a number of barges. During World War I, Robertson built two four-masted schooners for the Standard Oil Company, the *La Merced* and *Orinite*, as well as a five-masted schooner *Rose Mahoney*, and the barkentine *Monitor*. At the end of the war Robertson sold his interest in the yard to the Benicia Shipbuilding Company, which had him supervise the construction of three ferry-type steamers for the Emergency Fleet Corporation. When the shipyard was relocated to Alameda, California, in 1918, Robertson left Benicia. He was accidentally killed while moving a heavy piece of equipment in November 1927.

The world's first auto ferry, the *Charles Van Damme*, was built by James Robertson at the Robertson Shipyard in Benicia in 1916. Robertson, born in San Francisco in 1873, was apprenticed at age 13 at the Union Iron Works there. He later worked at the Hall Brothers Shipyard at Port Blakeley, Washington, studying at night to become a naval architect. The Union Iron Works sent Robertson to superintend the construction of caissons for dry-docks at the Imperial Russian Naval Yard in Vladivostok and he remained in Russia for three years. Robertson purchased Matthew Turner's shipyard in 1912. The *Charles Van Damme* was the last old-style ferry boat in service on San Francisco Bay and finished her long service on the Benicia-Martinez route in March 1955.

Russell Robertson, son of James Robertson, is shown on the deck of the schooner *Rose Mahoney*, c. 1915. The *Rose Mahoney* was 300 feet long and 50 feet wide; only 25 feet shorter and 3 feet narrower than the largest wooden sailing ship ever built. (Courtesy of James Robertson, son of Russell Robertson and grandson of James Robertson.)

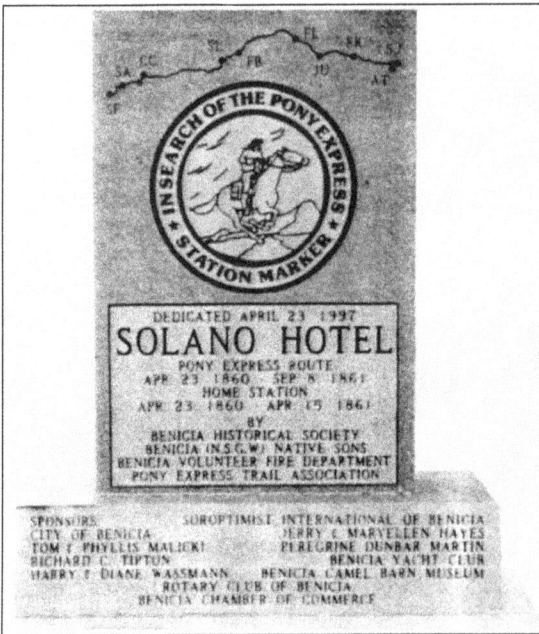

Transportation in Benicia's early days was via the horse, sailing ship, and ferry. A well-developed transportation system enabled industries to flourish. Benicia was a vital link in the famous Pony Express system. On April 23, 1860, Thomas J. Bedford, a 13-year-old Benicia resident, received the mailbag from William Hamilton, the first relay-rider, and took it across the Carquinez Strait to Martinez aboard the ferryboat *Carquinez*. There, he mounted a waiting horse and made the 25-mile ride in 1 hour and 59 minutes, which is reported to be the fastest time by any mail rider on any route. The final lap of this historic trip was made by ferryboat across the bay to San Francisco. In October 1861, the electric telegraph brought an early end to the heroic Pony Express, but a historical marker dedication was held on the centennial of the Pony Express. In 1997, another monument was placed in front of the Solano Hotel at First and E Streets, where the Pony Express station was located. The much-anticipated railroad service to Benicia was delayed by many setbacks until late 1878, when the city was finally connected to the transcontinental railroad. The new line was built at great cost due to the challenges of laying tracks through the marshes, but proved worth the effort when the town's manufacturers could transport their products more quickly and easily. The Central Pacific rerouted its main line through Benicia to take advantage of the 60-mile shortcut to San Francisco.

Southern Pacific's 3,549-ton ferryboat *Solano* made Benicia her home port in 1879. She was the largest ferryboat in the world at 424 feet long with a beam (width) of 116 feet. The *Solano's* rail deck had four parallel tracks that could carry two locomotives and 36 freight cars or 24 passenger cars. She transported an average of 30 trains a day between Benicia and Port Costa. The *Solano* is now being used as a breakwater in Antioch.

On October 14, 1911, William Howard Taft's reelection train transferred at Port Costa on the *Solano* en route to Benicia and then on to Sacramento.

At 433 feet long and 44,483 tons, the ferry *Contra Costa*, shown above being built at the Southern Pacific Shipyard at the foot of Peralta Street, Oakland, in 1914, was even larger than the *Solano*. These huge vessels were in service for 51 years—until 1930 when the railroad bridge was built. The whereabouts of the *Contra Costa* is unknown. The tug *Port Costa* is in the foreground of the above image.

The current railroad depot located at the end of First Street was originally built in Banta, California, in the mid-1890s and moved to Benicia in 1902. After the trains began traveling across the strait via the new railroad bridge in 1930 the building had various uses. Now restored, it serves as the Benicia Main Street office. Below, a Southern Pacific crew poses, *c.* 1920.

The railroad depot sits underwater during an overflow in 1950. By this time, the railroad tracks were long gone.

In 1930, the Southern Pacific Railroad built a bridge from Army Point in Benicia to Martinez. This put the railroad ferries out of business and industry began to move from the area at the end of First Street.

This view from the Benicia railroad yard looks east around 1923.

Railroad workers had their specific responsibilities. At top are the engineer and fireman. Below are three switchmen and the foreman. Larger crews were needed to put the trains on the railroad ferries, which at times would make 30 trips each day.

The long history of Benicia's ferry business began with city founder Robert Semple. Ferries would continue taking people and automobiles from Benicia to Martinez and San Francisco until 1962, when the Benicia to Martinez bridge was constructed. The last ferry to operate that line was the *Carquinez*.

The *Encinal* railroad ferry rode the waters between Oakland and San Francisco.

The *Encinal* ferry served as Spenger's Fish Grotto in Benicia. Paul E. Spenger (brother of Frank, of today's popular Berkeley restaurant) started his restaurant on the *James M. Donahue* in San Rafael in 1938. He later purchased the *Encinal*, towed it to Benicia and started Spenger's Restaurant there. The restaurant was a huge success, especially during World War II, and operated until the California State Park system took over this area and the *Encinal* was burned to the ground.

This happy group dines aboard Spenger's Fish Grotto, which seated 200.

The photograph at right shows the
beginning of construction of the first
auto bridge on the strait, the Carquinez
Bridge, which was completed in
1927. Joining the cities of Vallejo
and Crockett, the placing of the final
span can be seen on the opposite page.
A large crowd attended the opening
celebration in 1927 (below).

The Carquinez Bridge dedication took place on May 21, 1927. In 1958, another bridge was built beside the Carquinez, and in 2003 the third bridge was built and dedicated. The original bridge is slated to be torn down.

Three

PROMINENT BENICIANS AND THEIR HOMES

The Mizners were one of Benicia's most interesting pioneer families. After he arrived in California, Lansing Bond Mizner became a successful attorney in San Francisco, was elected to the state senate in 1865, joined William Robinson and Robert Semple in establishing a general merchandise company, tried to start a stage line and a Benicia-Marysville railway, and was instrumental in founding the Benicia Masonic Temple. Lansing and his wife, Ella, had high hopes for their sons, Addison and Wilson, but it seems they were always getting into mischief. Nevertheless, Wilson became known as a New York dilettante quipster and Broadway playwright, while Addison was an architect best known for his development of Boca Raton, Florida. The Mizners' only daughter, Mary Isabelle ("Min"), married Horace Blanchard Chase who became famous for his Stag's Leap Vineyards in Napa. The Mizner family, from left to right, included (front row): Addison Mizner (with tam); (second row) Lansing Bond Mizner, William Mizner (youngest son), Mary Isabelle "Min" Mizner, and Henry Mizner (with straw hat); (third row) Ella Watson Mizner, Lansing Mizner Jr., and William Mizner; (back row) Edgar Mizner. Wilson is not pictured.

The Mizners' tidy, two-story home was part of the growing town of Benicia. It was located near the corner of First and L Streets.

D.N. Hastings originally came to Benicia in 1850 and opened a successful butcher shop, which allowed him to return home to Massachusetts and bring his family to settle in Benicia in 1852. He combined his work as a butcher with raising livestock and became a very successful businessman and rancher, owning the Daly, O'Hara, Sulphur Springs, and Rocky Creek Ranches, but they ultimately proved inadequate to pay for "Hasting's Folly," the huge mansion he built to outdo his rivals L.B. Mizner and Miles Goodyear. Although not a politician, he held office as city trustee in the late 1870s.

The three-story mansion (shown above), built near St. Catherine's School in 1881, was the obsession of D.N. Hastings. After having an argument with Lansing Mizner and Andrew Goodyear, Hastings decided that he was going to "show them up" with this enormous residence. After a while, however, Hastings could no longer afford the mansion and it became known as "Hastings Folly." The last owners were the Dominican sisters from St. Catherine's who used it as a boy's dormitory. Below is the house shortly before it was razed as a fire hazard in 1937.

John Heenan, also known as the "Benicia Boy," became the first unofficial boxing champion in the United States. Heenan came to Benicia in 1852 at the age of 17 and worked in the Pacific Mail Steamship Company machine shops. Slinging a 20-pound sledge there helped to build his shoulders and biceps, making him a powerful and popular California fighter. In 1860, Heenan fought British champion Tom Sayers in a match that ended in a draw after 2 hours and 22 minutes.

John Heenan's home is no longer standing, but it is said to have been on the grounds of the old Benicia Barracks.

Stephen Vincent Benet was born in Bethlehem, Pennsylvania, in 1898 and was named after his grandfather. This photo was taken at the Benicia Arsenal in 1905, the year his father took over as commanding officer, serving from 1905 until 1911. Stephen, who was educated at boarding school, became a well-known poet, novelist, and short story writer. His *The Devil and Daniel Webster* was a long narrative poem that earned him a Pulitzer Prize in 1944, the year after his death. His son, Thomas Benet, is a member of the Benicia Historical Museum.

The Young Ladies Seminary was located on West H Street between First and Second Streets. It operated from 1852 to 1886, but truly flourished under the leadership of Mary Atkins Lynch. When Miss Atkins had to move to Honolulu for her health in 1866, the school was sold to Cyrus and Susan Mills. In 1878, Mary Atkins returned to the seminary as Judge John Lynch's wife. She brought the school statewide fame until her death in 1882. An impressive monument over her gravesite in the Benicia City Cemetery is a testament to her contributions in education at the Young Ladies Seminary.

Mary Farmer started teaching in 1889 at the West End Grammar School. She was revered as a teacher who treated all children equally and always gave the best she had. When she retired in 1922 after 33 years, she had taught 500 youngsters. An elementary school was named after her in 1976. In addition, a marker was put in the city park to honor this much admired teacher.

The Frank Stumm family picnics at Green Valley Falls in August 1908. Frank owned a fine jewelry store on First Street and was a much-respected photographer of Benicia history.

The Riddell-Fish House on West K Street was built around 1900. The home of Franklin and Henrietta Riddell Fish, this impressive Queen Anne Victorian was built with superior craftsmanship and was furnished with the English Aesthetic Movement in mind. It is still in excellent shape today due to restoration efforts in recent years. The home is privately owned and has been on the Benicia Historical Society home tour for a number of years.

Frank and Harriet Riddell Fish are shown here in early 1900s by the staircase of their home. Harriet was an accomplished artist who received medals for exhibits at the Mechanics Pavilion in San Francisco during the years 1881 and 1893. Her artwork could be found on screens, glass, wood, pottery, and ceramics, and she preferred to paint plein air landscapes. A friend of Susan Tolman Mills, who started Mills College in Oakland, Harriet taught art there for awhile but then became the first woman to open an art studio in San Francisco.

The Frisbee Walsh House on East L Street, shown here around 1850, was the home of Epiphania (Fannie) and her husband, John Frisbee. With its Gothic Revival architecture, it is historically one of the most important homes in Benicia. Gen. Mariano Vallejo's home, Lachryma Montis in Sonoma, is of similar architecture and it is thought that perhaps both of these homes were prefabricated on the East Coast and shipped around Cape Horn. Capt. John Walsh, a deputy collector for the port of Benicia, lived in the home from about 1850 until 1884. By the late 1980s, the exterior had been completely restored and it became a bed-and-breakfast inn. It is still privately owned.

The Crooks Mansion was built by J.H. Crooks in the late 1880s at the end of West Third and G Streets. Crook's brother, William, lived in the home for many years. William was president of the People's Bank in Benicia and served as the mayor from 1924 to 1940. The last of the Crook family to occupy the home was William's sister, Alice Crooks, who was a public school teacher. The home had fallen into disrepair by the late 1940s and was considered haunted by the locals. It has since been restored and is privately owned.

This is the c. 1910 home of Thomas Wright, the mayor of Benicia from 1944 to 1946. Wright was elected with councilmembers James Lemos, Michael FitzGerald, Paul Wetmore, and Albert Woodress. His wife, Erma, was the oldest living Benician at age 101 before she died in 1993.

City Manager James Walt and Mayor Thomas Wright are pictured with George Westerberg of Yuba Manufacturing, showing off the new dredge, *Franciscan*, built by Yuba.

The Benicia Monarchs beat the crack Vallejo all-star team in one of the fastest and most exciting games of the year, occurring sometime in the 1920s.

This photo shows the Pine Grocery Store, which was located on the first floor of the UPEC building on First Street. The gentleman in the photo is A.J. Pine. He bragged of his up-to-date goods at up-to-date prices. He still advertised, "Country goods [produce, eggs, milk, etc.] bought and sold."

Nikolai Petrovich Rezanov, a nobleman, was born in Saint Petersburg, Russia in 1764. He served in the imperial guard and in the court of Catherine the Great. Later he became the chief executive of the Shelekhov-Golikov Fur Company, one of several trade companies with outposts in the Alaskan territory. As Rezanov's political influence grew in the court and Russian senate, so did the fortunes of the fur company. Grief-stricken following the death of his wife, Anna, Rezanov left the imperial court to promote the first Russian circumnavigation of the earth from 1803 to 1806. Tsar Alexander I ordered Nikolai on an inspection tour of the Russian-American Company's colonies in the North Pacific. Rezanov found the settlers starving and beset by hostile Indians. Purchasing an American ship, he set sail for San Francisco (Yerba Buena) with a cargo of cloth, tools, muskets, and finery to barter for food. As the northern outpost for New Spain, San Francisco was off limits to all foreign ships and sailing into the bay was dangerous, but Rezanov dropped anchor nevertheless. Don Luis Antonio Argüello, who was in charge of the presidio during the absence of his father, the commandant, welcomed the Russians. They were invited to dinner where they met Senora Argüello and her three charming daughters, Anna Paula, Gertrudas Rudesinda, and Concepcion. (Early 19th-century portrait by an unknown artist; courtesy of Eve Iversen, author of *The Romance of Nikolai Rezanov and Concepcion Argüello*.)

This imagined portrait of Concepcion Argüello was painted by artist Lillie V. O'Ryan. Maria de la Concepcion Marcela Arquello was born on February 19, 1791, in California. She was spellbound by the dashing 42-year-old Rezanov. (Courtesy of Eve Iversen, author of *The Romance of Nikolai Rezanov and Concepcion Argüello*.)

The beautiful Concepcion, at 15 years of age, listened attentively as Rezanov, 42, told her about court life at Saint Petersburg, the richest and grandest court in Europe. She was impressed by the fair-complexioned Nikolai in his elegant navy uniform, and when Nikolai offered marriage, she accepted. They could not marry immediately because they were of different faiths: Concepcion, a Roman Catholic, and Nikolai, belonging to the Greek Orthodox Church. The padres would not perform the marriage without the approval of Rome and the czar, so the Russian suitor was granted a betrothal. The two exchanged gifts as they parted. Concepcion gave Nikolai a locket containing strands of her hair, and Nikolai gave her a chain with a jeweled cross attached. Rezanov was allowed to load his ship with California products and sailed away. This oil-on-canvas illustration of Conchita Argüello entitled *Beyond Memories*, was painted by Anatolio Sokoloff. (Courtesy of Alla and Igor Sokoloff.)

Shown here is the cover of the Russian historical novel *And the Ocean Roars* by Iuri Kachaev. On route to Russia Nikolai became ill. Neglecting his condition, he persisted in his effort to reach Saint Petersburg to obtain approval for his marriage from the czar. Tragically, he fell from his horse and died in Siberia on March 1, 1807. The inscription on the monument reads: "This monument was erected by the Russian-American Company on August 16, 1831, in memory of the unforgettable services rendered by Chamberlain Nikolai Petrovich Rezanov. Returning to Russia from America he passed away in the city of Krasnoyarsk." (Courtesy of Eve Iversen, author of *The Romance of Nikolai Rezanov and Concepcion Argüello*.)

69

Controversy exists as to how long Concepcion waited before she learned of Nikolai's death, but it is generally believed to have been six years. Beautiful and young, Concepcion had many suitors during that time, but she rejected them all, certain Nikolai would return to her. Much grieved when she learned of his death, Concepcion dedicated her life to charitable work, caring for the aged and infants, educating children, and nursing the sick. In 1850, the Dominican Sisters established Santa Catalina Convent in Monterey. Concepcion, now 60 years old, asked to be received into the order. In 1851, she received the Dominican habit and the name Sister Maria Dominica. The convent moved to Benicia in 1854 and its name was Anglicized to Saint Catherine's. Sister Dominica moved to Benicia in 1857. She died at the convent and was buried in the convent cemetery, though later interred at St. Dominic's Cemetery. Shown at left are Mother Marie de la Croix Goemaere, O.S.D., and Sister Mary Dominica Argüello (right). This is the only known portrait of Concepcion. (Courtesy of Eve Iversen, author of *The Romance of Nikolai Rezanov and Concepcion Argüello*.)

Shown at right is her headstone at St. Dominic's Cemetery in Benicia. One of the most fascinating women in California's history, she was known as "La Beata" because of the many charitable and religious acts she performed and as the first native California daughter to enter religious life. She was also known as Concha, the beloved fiancée of the Russian chamberlain Nikolai Rezanov. Their story captured the hearts of authors, painters, and historians.

Four

COMMUNITY

The first public school was established in what is now Benicia's city park in 1849. Sylvester Woodbridge was the first teacher.

St. Catherine's Academy was established in 1854 with Mother Mary Goemaere (pictured below) and the sisters of Santa Catalina convent in Monterey. The convent operated here, on the site of today's Solano Square, until 1889, when it moved to San Rafael to become Dominican College. The school taught only girls until 1902, when boys began attending. Subjects taught were quite extensive and included botany, tapestry, and orthography, among others. It closed in 1959.

Benicia Grammar School (Pacific Works School) was built on East K Street in 1881 and was co-educational, serving as a grammar school and a high school. This imposing three-story building operated until 1938.

Bishop John Henry Wingfield occupied this home on the site of St. Augustine's College from 1876 to 1898. He had come to the rescue of another Episcopalian school, St. Mary's of the Pacific, in 1876 by purchasing it and assuming its debt. He became that school's chancellor as well as its rector. St. Mary's closed its doors at the end of the 1884–1885 school year due to Wingfield's ill health. Though St. Augustine's closed in 1889, Wingfield continued to live in this house until 1898. It is now the only surviving building on the site of St. Augustine's and is privately owned.

Blake's Boarding School for Boys, founded in 1852, was one of the first schools in Benicia. Although it soon closed during the depression of 1854–1855, Blake's school was praised by John Fremont and others. It was reopened as the Benicia Collegiate Institute by Cornelius J. Flatt in 1857, and became famous for the law courses it offered. Its most renowned student was Joseph McKenna who became a Supreme Court justice. The Rev. Dr. James Lloyd Breck purchased the school in 1867 and re-named it the Missionary College of St. Augustine, an Episcopal boys' boarding school organized on a military model stressing discipline and moral and physical training. Breck died in 1877 and the school came under the supervision of Bishop John Wingfield, who lived in the house next to the school even after it closed in 1889. The house is the only building left on the site.

The Right Reverend William Ingraham Kip was the first Episcopal bishop of California.

St. Mary's of the Pacific was founded by Rev. James Lloyd Breck, an Episcopalian, in 1870. He felt that if the school could educate the girls, they would have the future mothers of the land and their children. The Mizner family was very involved in the school, with Lansing Bond Mizner on the board of trustees. Addison Mizner attended the school, as did four or five other boys. The most prominent student was novelist Gertrude Atherton.

Sulphur Springs School, shown here c. 1900, was built in the 1870s and operated until 1933 when students were transferred to Benicia. The school schedule at this school was slightly different than that of schools in the city, so that the children could help their parents during the harvest season. The school was located near Sky Valley, but at some point the building was moved to the area that is now just inside the entrance gates to Lake Herman. It is used as a utility building.

This 1950s photo shows Benicia High School in a building that was constructed in the mid-1920s on East L Street. The first class to graduate from that location in the school auditorium was the class of 1926. Previous graduations had been held at the Majestic Theatre. In the early 1960s the school was closed and a new one built on Military West. This school building was converted to Benicia City Hall.

St. Paul's Episcopal Church was established in 1854 and the church was built in 1860. Shipwrights from the Pacific Mail Steamship Company built it in the Gothic Revival style with a ceiling resembling the inverted hull of a wooden ship. Additions and changes have been made over the years. The structure on the left was a Sunday school, built in 1882. It is now the guild hall.

St. Dominic's Church, shown here in the 1970s, was built in 1890. The first building constructed for the Dominican seminary in 1854 was a small, wooden church (that was never completed) under the leadership of Rev. Archbishop Joseph Alemany. The seminary moved in 1923 to St. Albert's College in Oakland. St. Dominic's opened a grammar school in the former St. Catherine's Academy, which closed in 1959.

The Dominican archibishop in San Francisco, Joseph Sadoc Alemany, had blessed and christened St. Dominic's Church in 1854. It was he who invited Mother Mary Goemaere to bring her sisters of Santa Catalina convent from Monterey to Benicia to form St. Catherine's. He also brought Sister Mary Dominica into the order in 1851.

The First Congregational Church on West J Street was built in 1868. It lost its tower in 1923 when it was hit by lightning. It is now a private residence. A new church was built in the mid-1900s and is located on West Second Street. This photo was likely taken in late 19th century.

The St. Dominic's Cemetery began in the 1890s when the sisters interred at St. Catherine's cemetery were moved here along with the graves of the Dominican fathers from St. Dominic's monastery cemetery. The most prominent gravesite here is of Sister Mary Dominica. This photo shows museum curator Harry Wassmann at a ceremony honoring her.

This building began as a Methodist church that was dedicated in 1882. Due to poor attendance and lack of finances it closed around 1915. It was used as an antiques shop and is now a salon and spa.

Benicia loves a parade! Everyone came out to watch this Fourth of July parade, c. 1900. Notice the dirt streets.

Some former homes and churches have been used for different purposes than originally intended. This Methodist church on West J Street operated as an antique shop for many years; the building now houses a health spa.

Benicia's City Cemetery was shown on the first map of Benicia in 1847. Many well-known Benicians are buried there, including Capt. E.H. Von Pfister, Miles Goodyear, Capt. Dillingham, and Mary Atkins Lynch to name a few. Shown here is the headstone of Capt. E.H. Von Pfister, the first merchant in Solano County. The cemetery has several divisions such as Catholics, pioneers, Masons, Portuguese, etc.

The oldest U.S. military post cemetery, located in the former Benicia Arsenal grounds, was established in 1849. One Italian and eight German prisoners of war are buried there as well as a horse and a dog named Sgt. Tuffy, who was born in the early 1940s at the Benicia Arsenal. The cemetery is well maintained.

Locals gathered for a Benicia Chamber of Commerce reorganization and expansion campaign, c. 1915. Among those attending are Milo Passalacqua, Roland Wilson, Dorothy Drew, Ellen Foley, William Dykes, Frank Hoffman, and Jeanne Wassmann.

This May Day celebration was held in 1923 at the Pometta Ranch. The ranch was owned by Alma Pometta, who became postmistress in 1936.

Bathers enjoy Berletti's Beach c. 1900.

A Portuguese celebration parade passes in front of St. Dominic's Church in 1908.

The State Theatre, which was originally called the Majestic and is now the Majestic again, is shown here with O'Grady's Drug Store on the corner.

The Majestic Theatre on First Street was built in 1920 and used as a silent film and vaudeville theatre. It was renamed the State Theatre in the 1940s and showed movies. By the 1980s, it had seen various uses such as a children's theatre and a church. Recently it has hosted live entertainment. Many Benicians think of their first date when they see this theatre.

The interior of the Majestic Theatre was decorated in mulberry, teal, and gold. Leather seats provided room for 600 patrons. The original proscenium arch remains.

Steve De Benedetti and friends look like they are enjoying this job, hanging historical signs in 1949 at the various historical sights in Benicia.

In this photo, a Benicia High School women's baseball team in 1921 receives a championship trophy from the Solano County Athletic Association. From left to right are (front row) Mary Joseph, Marie Foss, Geraldine Silva, Mary Murray, and Winona ?; (back row) Hope Peters, Viola Peterson, Florence Clymo, Miss McCully, Lucy Chiotti, and Evelyn Wilson.

This photo shows the Benicia High School track team in the 1920s or 1930s. School sports were important activities that kept Benicia youth busy.

Remember when America had paper collections? Here the Benicia Boy Scouts are working hard putting newspaper into railroad cars in the 1940s. This activity was a popular fundraiser after World War II.

At left, Sen. Luther Gibson shows off his catch here in the 1960s. He was owner of the Gibson Horseshoe Duck Club. Below, a group of women employees were guests of the Teal Duck Club in 1934.

A parade is on the march with the city and civilian band on First Street in 1917.

Oldtimers in 1949 participate in performing a mock court scene. These kinds of events were popular for many years.

Groundbreaking of the James Lemos pool took place in the 1950s.

Swimmers line up at the James Lemos pool in the 1950s—a popular recreation for Benicians of the time.

Five

U.S. Benicia Barracks and Arsenal

Gen. Persifor (Persifer) Smith reported to the War Department in Washington, D.C., that Benicia was an ideal place for a post, including an armory and arsenal. In 1849, he negotiated with Robert Semple for a military reservation of approximately 300 acres. The military reservation was located one mile east of Benicia and the army built three installations there: U.S. Benicia Barracks, a quartermaster's depot, and the arsenal. This c. 1860 railway survey print shows the U.S. military post in Benicia.

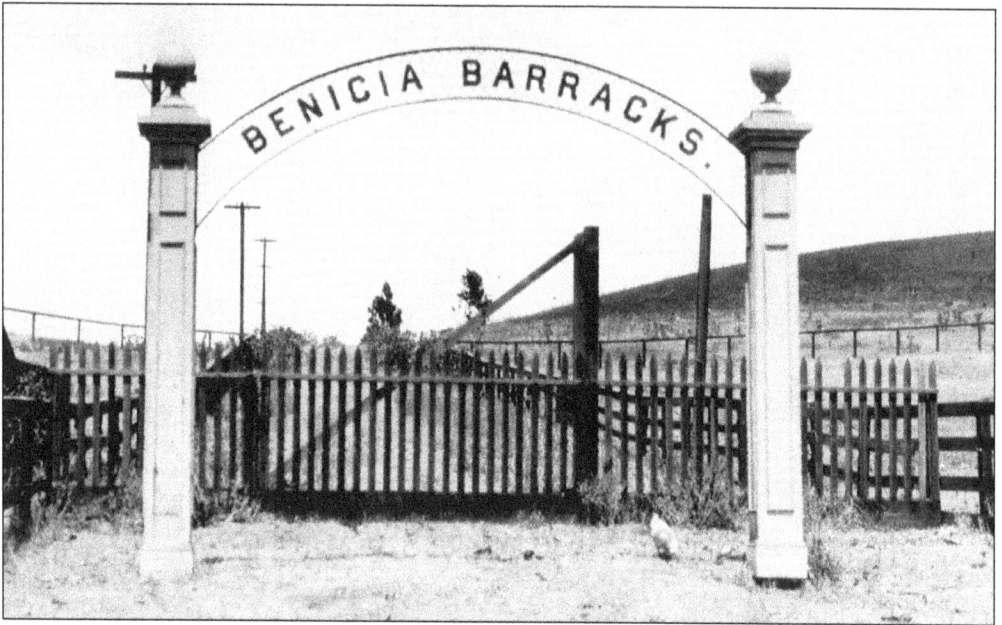

The U.S. Benicia Barracks occupied 99.5 acres in the northwest corner of the donated grounds. On April 30, 1849, Brevet Lt. Colonel Silas Casey of the 2nd Infantry and approximately 135 officers and men disembarked on the government land and established the "post at Point near Benicia, California." Units of the 1st Dragoons and the 3rd Artillery rode out from there on defensive sweeps up and down the coast quelling Indian uprisings and depredations against miners and settlers. During the Civil War, the California Volunteers assembled at the barracks were equipped with military gear, and given military training before embarking for the East. The barracks were in use until the end of the Spanish-American War and deactivated in 1908. In 1922, all the barracks buildings except the hospital were destroyed by fire. The land was absorbed by the Benicia Arsenal in 1924.

Lt. Col. Silas Casey played a significant role in the military operations in the Pacific Northwest. During the Indian Wars of 1855–1856, he showed compassion toward the native populations who were often the victims in altercations with miners and discretion in representing the interest of the United States in the boundary dispute with England. In addition to maintaining law and order in this Western outpost, he conducted topographical and geographical surveys of the area. During the Civil War, Casey served in the Peninsula Campaign, was promoted to brigadier general of volunteers in 1861 and major general in 1862. He spent the rest of the war as an administrator and commanded a provisional brigade in the defense of Washington, D.C., for a period before retiring in 1868. Casey died in Brooklyn, New York, in 1882 and was buried at his family farm in North Kingstown, Rhode Island.

Military personnel are shown here at the post hospital, the first military hospital built in the West (1856), constructed of native sandstone blocks. Casualties from troop skirmishes with Indian marauders as far away as the Northwest Territory were brought here for treatment. During World War II, the building served as the post chapel. The hospital remained in use through the Korean War.

This image shows the residence of the Benicia Barracks' commanding officer.

Ulysses S. Grant was the most famous American ever to soldier at Benicia Barracks, where he served as regimental quartermaster, 4th Infantry. Grant and the 4th Infantry sailed from New York on July 5, 1852, and arrived in California after a perilous trip across the isthmus in which dozens in the party were killed and Quartermaster Grant served as "a ministering angel" to those struck down by cholera, poisonous plants, and tainted water. Grant lost his close friend, Major John Gore, who was suddenly stricken with cholera while playing poker. Grant barely mentioned Benicia in his two-volume memoir, saying only: "My regiment spent a few weeks at Benicia Barracks and then was ordered to Fort Vancouver." Grant had been officially posted to Benicia for temporary duty on a court-martial panel, although the court-martial was called off at the last minute. Grant eventually became Lincoln's Civil War commander-in-chief and, later, president of the United States.

Brig. Gen. George Stoneman, shown here c. 1862, served as a lieutenant at Benicia Barracks in 1851. A member of the Benicia Masonic Lodge, he was also the drum barracks commander in 1869 and 1870, served in the regular army as colonel and brevet rank of major-general and retired in 1871. Stoneman became the 15th governor of California, serving from 1883 to 1887.

The Benicia Arsenal, the first U.S. Ordnance supply activity in California, was established by Army Brevet Capt. Charles P. Stone in August 1851 to receive, store, ship, and maintain arms for military activities on the Pacific Coast and to respond to national emergencies. The installation also repaired equipment, disposed of damaged material, and produced and tested ammunition for the army. It supplied survey and exploration parties and military posts, which maintained peace and security on the Western frontier. The arsenal personnel were both military and civilian and were usually commanded by an army colonel. This image shows the Benicia Arsenal gates in the early part of the 20th century.

Charles Pomeroy Stone (1824–1887) was born in Greenfield, Massachusetts, and graduated from the U.S. Military Academy. He was given orders at age 26 to establish a permanent ordinance supply depot on the San Francisco Bay. On August 15, 1851, Captain Stone arrived at the Golden Gate with a cargo of muskets, swords, subsistence supplies, tarpaulins, lumber, and "prairie carriages" or covered wagons. Stone was in command of Benicia Arsenal and chief of ordnance of the Division and Department of the Pacific until 1856. In 1865, General Stone was appointed superintendent of the Dover Mining Company in Virginia. After accepting a commission in the Egyptian Army, he created a typographical bureau and became a member of the Egyptian Institute in Cairo. Upon his return to the United States he became engineer-in-chief for the construction of the pedestal of Bartholdi's statue of "Liberty Enlightening the World," and acted as grand marshal in the ceremony that accompanied the dedication of the statue, now known as the Statue of Liberty.

This *c.* 1856 army photograph of the Benicia Arsenal buildings shows the camel barns on the right, headquarters on the left, and some Benicia Barracks buildings in the upper left corner. The camel barns, consisting of two warehouses (buildings no. 7 and no. 9) and an engine house (center), were the first permanent arsenal structures and were built from local sandstone quarried on the site. Their name and notoriety comes from a short-lived "military camel experiment" conducted by the U.S. Army, when 37 camels were auctioned there.

The powder magazine (building no. 10) was built in 1857. The second of two almost identical powder magazines, this one has slightly more elaborate decoration. It was built of finely-worked sandstone by French craftsmen who were brought to the arsenal especially for the construction of this and other sandstone buildings. The walls are four-foot thick solid stone, the ceilings are vaulted, and the interior Corinthian pillars are hand carved. There were special rules and regulations for the magazine, with Orders No. 37 reading

1. Never to be opened except in presence of our officer or some non-commissioned officer specially designated by the commanding officer; 2. Whoever enters a magazine must take off his shoes, or put on slippers over them and leave outside his cane, sword, sabre, or any other thing about him which can produce a spark; 3. Whenever a magazine is opened, a guard must be stationed near with orders to allow no one to pass without permission. The sentry must be armed with a sabre or bayonet, never his fire-arm.

As for the sandstone: in a memo dated January 1852, Captain Stone mentioned the excellent local building stone. When no bricks or cement arrived from the East, Stone and his successor, Capt. Franklin Callender, simply ran the sandstone foundation blocks all the way to the roofs of the seven structures. Thus the handsome and sturdy stone walls of the Benicia Arsenal were the result of a bureaucratic oversight in Washington, D.C. (National Archives collection, Cartographic Division, Record Group 156.)

This detail of the sculpture above the doorway of the powder magazine showing an eagle on a cannon is of remarkably high quality and is reputably the work of French immigrant John Gomo.

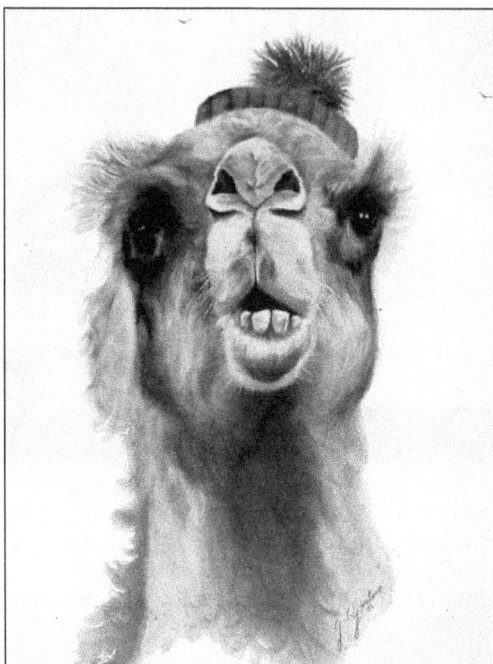

Camels were once a part of Benicia's colorful history. Benicia turned out to be the last station for the camels during the army's military camel experience. (Drawing by Gil Garitano, 1972. Courtesy of Todd Lieber, former intern at the Benicia Historical Museum.)

A Bactrian camel embarks on a barge in Smyrna, Turkey, in this contemporary sketch by Gwynne Harris Heap, the civilian advisor of the expedition. (National Archives & Record Service, Washington, D.C.) In 1855, Jefferson Davis, as Secretary of War, persuaded Congress to appropriate $30,000 to import camels to the United States to serve as transportation in the effort to develop the Southwest desert. A navy store-ship sailed to the eastern Mediterranean and brought back a mixed herd of light and speedy Dromedaries from Egypt, which had one hump, and the heavier and slower two-humped Bactrian camels from Turkey. All but one of the 33 camels survived the three-month voyage. Another load of 44 camels were later transported to Indianola, Texas, and then driven to Camp Verde, where the first and only U.S. Camel Corps was born. Few soldiers had any appreciation of the camels' potential or an understanding of their handling, and it was decided in 1863 to close down the camel corps and sell its assets—which for the most part were the camels. The camels were brought to Benicia.

In January 1864 the camels arrived at the U.S. Benicia Arsenal and a corral was built at the so-called Camel Barns Complex of the U.S. Benicia Arsenal. On February 26, 1864, an auction was held, selling off 37 camels (some publications report the sale of 36 camels). Congress's initial $30,000 investment brought back the sum of $1,945, less the two-and-a-half percent commission to the auctioneer. Deputy Quartermaster General Lt. Col. E.B. Babbitt reported to his superiors that "the amount of the sale was less than I had hoped for, but when I consider that they are absolutely unserviceable for any governmental purpose, I cannot but regard their sale at even a less price as a decided benefit to the United States." Those camels that were not sold were turned loose in the Great American Desert, and reports of camel sightings in the desert were common well into the 20th century. One vivid account came for a group of freight haulers who bedded down for the night on the bank of the Verde River and whose sighting gave rise to the famous Red Ghost story that roamed the desert for more that 25 years. (Courtesy of Del Lacey.)

Gretchen Burgess was the winner of two consecutive camel races held in Benicia and organized by the Benicia Historical Museum. Camel history continues even today.

The City of Benicia leased the camel barns and powder magazine to the Benicia Historical Museum, which held its grand opening on May 19, 1985.

Lt. Col. James Walker Benet was the commanding officer of the Benicia Arsenal and assigned as Armament Officer, Western Department, from 1905 to 1911. He was born in Richmond, Kentucky, in 1857 and graduated from West Point in 1880 and from the Army Artillery School in 1884. He commanded the Ordnance Training Corps, Camp Hancock, in Augusta, Georgia, from June 1918 to February 1919 and took over command of the Watervliet Arsenal in March 1919. A member of the Loyal Legion, he died in 1928 and was buried in Arlington National Cemetery.

This c. 1878 lithograph of the Benicia Arsenal shows the machine shop (building no. 55) and the blacksmith shop (building no. 57) in the foreground. Building no. 56 is not completed. In the background are the commandant's residence and the lieutenant's quarters with the formal parade grounds and the flagpole between them. The arsenal—in operation from 1851 to 1964—opened and closed during periods of intense activity due to the wars in which the United States was engaged. Between the times of conflict there was a quiet period when the installation's principal work was as a proving ground for the testing of gunpowder being manufactured on the Pacific Coast. The era also marked a change in the construction of arsenal operational buildings, the use of native sandstone being replaced by brick with sandstone trim. A good description of the whole military reservation at this time was recorded in a letter of January 15, 1860, written by soldier Eugene Bandel to his parents:

> The Arsenal consist of an officer's house, two large storehouses; two powder magazines, a laboratorium (where cartridges are made); a long wooden building containing the wheelwright's shop; armory and saddlery; a smithy; quarter for the soldiers; guardhouse and a paint shop; and, finally, close to the water's edge, a number of smaller buildings which are in use as homes for the married soldiers.

The arsenal's second commander, Franklin D. Callender, requested in June 1857 that a sum of $50,000 be set aside for a new storehouse. In one of his letters to the Ordnance Office in Washington he explained that he wanted a building with towers on all four corners to be used for flank defense in the case of attack by local citizens. The clock tower, shown here in 1891, was built in 1859. The long, thin slots around the building were designed for use in rifle practice, while the front and rear openings were for cannon fire. The walls were made of two-foot thick sandstone. The clock tower is considered the only 19th-century gothic stone fortress in the United States.

103

On October 18, 1912, fire destroyed the third floor and rear tower.

During remodeling following the fire, the third floor and rear tower were eliminated. The large American-made Seth Thomas clock in the front tower was installed as a memorial to Col. Julian McAllister, who was commander of the Benicia Arsenal for 25 years. The clock tower has served as a munitions depot, chapel, and as a National Guard Armory. Today, its upper level serves as a community activity center and is a popular and frequently used facility.

The first occupant of the Benicia Arsenal commandant's residence, seen here from the west sometime between 1946 and 1950, was Julian McAllister, who commanded the arsenal between 1860 and 1886, with the exception of two years between 1864 and 1866, when he was called east to help with the defense of New York City in the Civil War. Born in New York City in 1823, McAllister was the son of a prominent Savannah, Georgia, family. His brother, Ward McAllister, was the leader of New York society and another brother, Hall McAllister, a prominent San Francisco lawyer. Julian McAllister was active in the planning and construction of St. Paul's Episcopal Church and his presence in Benicia made the arsenal a major social and cultural center for the town. He built many structures at the arsenal, including the commanding officer's house (building no. 28), an impressive 20-room mansion with 14-foot ceilings. When the army pulled out of the arsenal in the early 1960s, the commandant's quarters began a slow process of deterioration. The City of Benicia and dedicated residents are determined to restore this magnificent building to its former glory.

This interior view of the commandant's residence was taken in the 1940s or 1950s.

The lieutenant's quarters were built in 1861. The officers standing in front of the lieutenant's quarters c. 1940, from left to right, are Lt. Col. F.D. Pearce, Lt. Col. P.F. Harper, and Maj. W. Bloch. Built in 1861, the lieutenant's quarters have been restored by its current owner. Today the building is known as the Jefferson Street Mansion and serves the community as a charming site for weddings, corporate functions, and private parties.

Four women wait in front of the lieutenant's quarters.

After the Civil War, the arsenal continued its mission as principal ordnance distribution depot west of the Rocky Mountains. However, because there were no adequate shop facilities, the chief of ordnance urged the secretary of war to obtain appropriations for the construction of much-needed shop structures. The first permanent shop, completed in 1876, was a one-story brick building with stone trim that was used as a blacksmith and carpenter shop. This facility was the first of a beautiful trio of buildings; the second, erected the following year, was a two-story brick and stone building remarkable for the splendor of its arched windows and doorways and outlines of stone blocks. The third building was built in 1884 and was used as a machine shop.

Between 1880 and 1890 an additional function was given to the Benicia Arsenal: testing powder manufactured on the West Coast. A site near Benicia Army Point was selected for this operation; the army point was a strategic place to control the key passageway of the Carquinez Strait and access to the gold mines. Later, in 1930, the Southern Pacific Railroad bridges between Benicia Army Point and Martinez were built.

In late summer 1862, a group of Californians, most of them originally from the East Coast, contacted Governor Andrews of Massachusetts and proposed to raise 100 volunteers to form a separate company in a cavalry regiment currently being raised in Massachusetts. The governor agreed, with the condition that the Californians would provide their own uniforms and equipment. Officially they became Company "A" of the 2nd Massachusetts Cavalry, but they were more popularly known as the "California Hundred." A replica of the "California Hundred" flag is displayed here at the military exhibition in the powder magazine. (Courtesy of Jeff Matthews.)

Civil War weaponry on display at the powder magazine includes a pennon lance (in front). Pennon lances were made at the Benicia Arsenal during the Civil War, and a statement of fabrications shows that as of June 30, 1865, Benicia Arsenal had manufactured 274 lances, 275 arm slings, 275 flags, and 275 sockets for the lances. (Courtesy of Jim Kanne.)

The 1888 Independence Day band included, from left to right, (front row) W. Shaw, James Smith, H. Starky, Joseph Hern, Jack Heferman, and Jack Kennedy; (back row) W. Starr, Albert Myers, George Godley, Nicholas Starr, unidentified, William Beak, George Connors, and Martin Weir.

After the United States entered World War I on April 6, 1917, activity increased at the arsenal and continued for three of four more years with the repair and disposition of large amounts of ordnance supplies. The number of civilians working at the installation increased during the period from 45 to a peak of 300 workers. During the war they supplied troops in the mobilization camps of Lewis, Fremont, and Kearny, as well as at various posts in the Western Department. Arsenal shops serviced all weapons for the 91st Division before that unit shipped out for overseas duty in Europe. Shown here is a World War I uniform on display in the powder magazine.

This photograph of a group of Benicia High School students is from the collection of Richard B. Maurer, shown here with arms crossed in the top right center of the top row of boys. He graduated in 1920 and worked in building no. 9 assembling 75-mm shells during World War I, in the summer of 1918.

General John Pershing (left) visited the Benicia Arsenal on January 24, 1920. General Pershing is shown with Colonel O'Hern on the steps of the arsenal headquarters. During World War I, General Pershing was the commander of the American Expeditionary Force in Europe. After the war he was promoted to general of the armies, a position previously held only by George Washington.

After World War I, merchant vessels were "laid up" in Southampton Bay and remained there from 1919 to 1932. Two of the vessels were concrete hull ships—one of them the *Palo Alto*, now beached at Sea Cliff State Park in Aptos.

Throughout World War II military supplies were loaded aboard liberty ships at Benicia docks. During the war the arsenal's responsibilities were defined as (a) retail issue of assembled tanks, small arms, and fire control; (b) retail issue of parts, supplies, tools, and equipment for tanks, artillery, small arms, and fire control equipment; (c) clip, belt, and link small arms ammunition; (d) transshipment of ammunition of all classes; (e) overhaul and modification of small arms, artillery, fire control, tanks, and full-truck self-propelled mounts; (f) training of civilian personnel.

The liberty ship *Jeremiah O'Brien* was laid up in the mothball fleet and, later, was the only one to leave the mothball fleet under her own power. *Jeremiah O'Brien* sailed to Normandy in 1994 to celebrate the 50th anniversary of D-Day; the only ship to have been present there both in 1944 and 1994.

During the critical labor shortages of World War II, women constituted approximately 49 percent of the civilian employee force at the arsenal. Here, Bernice Chiotti inspects a rifle in the small arms shop at Benicia Arsenal in 1943. Rifles, machine guns, and other weapons were serviced there.

A Christmas party was held at the small arms shop at Benicia Arsenal during World War II, c. 1942.

In November 1943, Colonel Paul Rutten, the arsenal commander, grew tired of hearing complaints of how "arsenal-based" hawks were killing chickens and other small domestic animals in the local community. To correct the situation, Rutten assigned Sgt. Woodrow Taylor and Cpl. Alec Brown, shown here, to use short-range carbine rifles and "carefully" thin out the hawk population. (No "explosion" was noted at the arsenal during the operation!)

Three men from the Arsenal Military Police detachment relax in their quarters on the second floor of an enlisted men's barracks. While the arsenal's gates and fence lines were policed by civilian guards, MPs and Anti-Aircraft Artillery units were rushed to the installation for other protective purposes. In April 1942, the Western Defense Command directed the district engineer to construct cantonment-type buildings in the old Benicia Barracks area to house such military personnel.

This mannequin is dressed in the World War II uniform of ordnance officer Captain Dyer. The flaming cannonball emblem of the U.S. Army Ordnance Corps is on the wall. The uniform is on display in the powder magazine as part of the military exhibit at the Benicia Historical Museum.

The machine shop and tank shop at the Benicia Arsenal operated during the Korean War. It is seen here in 1950.

Jim Mortensen was 19 when he served in the Korean War. His uniform is on display at the Benicia Historical Museum and is dedicated to all military personnel who served in the Korean War. There is no military uniform more recognizable than "Marine dress blues."

This March 2, 1945 view of Benicia Military Cemetery from a hill on the east side shows the nearly completed north addition of the cemetery. The south addition is underway, but not completed. The cemetery was founded in 1849 and may be the oldest U.S. military post cemetery in the Pacific states. The last burials occurred in 1958. Besides soldiers and civilians, including women and children, eight German and one Italian prisoners of war were buried at the cemetery during World War II. Approximately 400 German and 250 Italian POWs were brought to a branch POW camp at the Benicia Arsenal to help alleviate the labor shortage there. Three pets are also buried at the cemetery. (Photo by Robert Dyer.)

Four soldiers with flags walk through Benicia Military Cemetery in 1983.

Corp. K.J. Broder, Colonel Rutten's chauffeur, prepares to remove his old corporal stripes and sew on new sergeant's stripes.

Col. W.B. Moats, commanding officer of the Benicia Arsenal from 1958 to 1959, is shown here with John Baldwin, U.S. congressman for Solano and Contra Costa Counties.

118

In February 1959, Gary Widman was promoted from second lieutenant to first lieutenant by Colonel Moats, commanding officer of the Benicia Arsenal. Later, Gary Widman served in the White House during the terms of Presidents Nixon and Ford.

Col. and Mrs. Lewis Nickerson attend the Christmas ball at the Benicia Arsenal Officer's Quarters, c. 1949. Nickerson was commander of the Benicia Arsenal from 1935 to 1938 and again from 1946 to 1950.

Col. John P. Sherden, commanding officer, presents an award to Lt. Col. Verne M. Jensen, executive officer at the Benicia Arsenal, 1963. Maj. Leonard Auger is in the center.

American Legion Post 101 of Benicia, under the direction of Comdr. Frank Fiore, presented a United States flag to Benicia Barracks No. 2125 World War I Veterans in the Veterans Memorial Hall on September 22, 1960. Shown, from left to right, are E.W. Crozer (adjutant of Benicia Barracks No. 2125 World War I Veterans), Frank Fiore, and Rudy Quandt, commander of the new barracks group.

120

This U.S. Army Ordnance Insignia plaque was presented to Frank Fiore, commander of the American Legion Post 101, by Colonel Wells, commanding officer of the Benicia Arsenal (1959–1961) for safe keeping.

Col. Francis G. Hall was the commanding officer of the Benicia Arsenal from 1953 to 1955.

Col. W.B. Moats was the commanding officer of the Benicia Arsenal from 1958 to 1959.

Col. John P. Sherden was the commanding officer of the Benicia Arsenal from 1959 to 1961.

The official flag take-down is performed in front of the headquarters of the Benicia Arsenal, March 31, 1964. The Benicia Arsenal was the first arsenal on the West Coast and its soldiers and supplies held the Western territories together by providing military support for everything from early Indian conflicts to the Korean War. The number of civilian workers on base skyrocketed to nearly 10,000, including 700 Benicians. The rest came from nearby communities like Oakland, Napa, Vallejo, and Richmond.

Frank Fiore, American Legion Post 101, received the flag as the Benicia Arsenal closed on March 31, 1964. Returning from World War II, Frank started work at the arsenal at $1 an hour. Rumors of arsenal closure were circulating. "The rumors were there in '48 and '49. But the Korean conflict saved us. Then, in '51 and '52, the Nike missiles and radar era came into the picture and that saved us, too. The government sent half a dozen men from every Army installation in the country to get involved in the missiles. We were in the pioneer days of electronics, and converted over to maintenance and repair of the Nike, AJAX, and Hercules missiles," said Frank Fiore. "By the time they closed it in 1964, there were about 3,200 people left."

During its 113 years of existence, the Benicia Arsenal contributed to the greatness of America's military heritage.

The arsenal closure meant a new start for the City of Benicia. In 1963, city attorney John Bohn helped Benicia work out the details for the acquisition of the arsenal properties and the eventual lease of the park to Benicia Industries. The master lease between the city and Benicia Industries was signed on January 7, 1963. Among the first major employers to locate in the park were Weldon Leather Company and Ace Hardware. Humble Oil and Refining Company (Exxon, Valero Refining Company) began construction of its refinery in 1966 and has operated at the site since 1969. Pictured fifth from the left is James Lemos, the mayor of Benicia. "The majority of the 2,400 people at the Arsenal were Benicians, and local residents forecast economic disaster for the city. But business leaders and elected officials would not let Benicia die," wrote Bill Tanner, former public relations manager of the Valero Refining Company–California in 2003.

This aerial view shows the Benicia Industrial Park, located off the Carquinez Strait, in 1976. Note the body of water in the center of the photo. This was Pine Lake, the reservoir for the Benicia Arsenal, which was located off Park Road, north of Highway 780. The camel barns and powder magazine, which are now occupied by the Benicia Historical Museum, are located to the right of the lake. The area above Pine Lake is the beginning of the Exxon Refinery, which is now owned by Valero Refining Company-California. In the lower part of the shoreline is the Port of Benicia. Parked along the shore are the automobiles that were once shipped to the port on a regular basis. In the water to the upper right is the Suisun Bay Reserve Fleet of naval ships that have been located there since 1945.

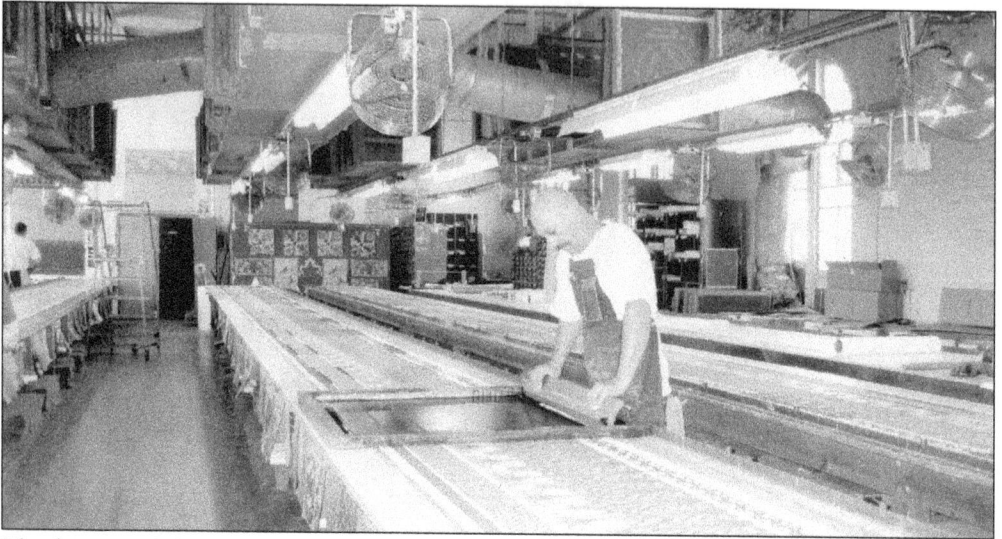

The history of the arsenal continues with the reuse of its building by many businesses and private organizations. In 1979, Bradbury & Bradbury Art Wallpapers started their small hand-printing studio in Benicia. Today the company has an international reputation for fine reproductions of wallpapers from the 19th and early 20th centuries. Bradbury wallpapers have been hung in the Metropolitan Museum and produced the romantic backdrops in such movies as *Hook* and *Dracula*. A unique mail-order design service creates elaborate Victorian ceilings for clients in the United States, Europe, and Australia. In this photo, Scott Corral, a printer at Bradbury & Bradbury Art Wallpapers, works on a lane.

Bonnie Weidel was the founding president of the first art organization in Benicia, the Benicia Community Arts, to respond to the national effort to advance the arts and art education in June 1980. In August 1986, she moved to her studio into this former arsenal building, which was added to the machine shop to make and test weapons in the 1940s. What was once an arsenal of weapons is today an arsenal of businesses, arts, and history.

Here are the Benicia-Martinez bridges: Railroad Bridge, Highway 680/780 bridge, and the new bridge under construction. Bridges, ferries, boats, and highways brought you to Benicia. You made your journey into this early California town and experienced our story. Take time now, imagine the sound of lapping waves on the Carquinez Strait as you choose your pathway to depart.

Visit us at
arcadiapublishing.com

www.ingramcontent.com/pod-product-compliance
Lightning Source LLC
Chambersburg PA
CBHW080559110426
42813CB00006B/1344